21 Days of Prayers

An Individual and Group Process To Transform Your Prayer Life

Cedrick D. Bridgeforth

For everyone who has ever uttered a prayer.

CONTENTS

HOW TO USE THIS BOOK

This book is a primer for any person seeking to integrate prayer into their lifestyle and for leaders seeking to transform or launch a prayer ministry. This is a 21-Day process with daily and weekly reflections alongside each prayer.

The Prayers
The prayers are personal, introspective and investigative in nature – trusting each individual will commit to doing real soul searching each day. The prayers are real prayers prayed by the author and are deeply personal. They are shared in this medium as a way of challenging others to go deeper in their personal prayer life and to be a bit selfish and vulnerable from time-to-time while communing with God. None of the prayers complete without additions and further reflections.

As participants become more comfortable, they may begin expanding each prayer to include their own salutations, perspectives, petitions and thanksgivings. The goal of this process is for each participant to reflect upon what is on the page, and to also develop and expand their own understanding of prayer from a deeply personal space. Incorporating a prayer journal will also deepen the experience while expanding into another spiritual discipline.

Group/Partner Process
If this book is used as a Group/Partner Process, there is a weekly guide for Days 7, 14, and 21. The "Guide" allows for those present to reflect upon what has been

experienced while also anticipating what is to come.

Personal Reflections and Affirmations
The Personal Reflections and Affirmations are there for continued thought, exploration and application throughout the day and week. They may also be used in discussion with accountability or prayer partners. It must be noted that as the Weekly Reflections will not be relevant to every group, each prayer will not be relevant to every person.

Use of "Amen"
This volume does not include any complete or finite prayers. Each prayer is a beginning of a stream of thoughts, emotions, expectations, experiences, hopes and unmentionables that cannot be bound or concluded on these pages. Each participant will expand and explore these prayers differently and may take issue with various assertions and assumptions assumed or discovered to be in the text. That activity alone connotes a lack of closure or finality. Therefore, the author neglected to use "Amen" so that each participant would feel invited to make each prayer their own.

Other Uses
The prayers in this book can also be used as discussion starters when small groups or classes gather. If a leader wishes to bring a team together and have them become more trusting and authentic with each other, this 21-Day process will serve the leader and team in their pursuits.

Cover Photo

Cover photo taken by Cedrick Bridgeforth. The photo is of a centerpiece at an event hosted by the Tongan Fellowship of Santa Ana United Methodist Church, a multi-site, multi-ethnic congregation with worship and cultural ministries in Tagalog, English, Khmer, Spanish and Tongan.

DAY 1
WISDOM

I pray that everyone I know will be gifted with wisdom and strength. I pray for all of us because we need wisdom and strength to bring all our burdens and misgivings to you.

Give us wisdom to let go of the things that keep us from growing closer to you. Give us strength to let go of the things that keep us from growing closer to each other. Give us wisdom and strength to clear our spiritual ears and to widely and unconditionally open our hearts. Give us wisdom to trust the truths of your word until our change comes and your mission for us is fulfilled.

We want and need all these things so we can become better acquainted with you and your voice. We want and need all these things so we can better acclimate to the direction you have charted for our lives.

Give us what we need to make it through this day and to experience at least one more victory that glorifies your name. Give us fortitude of character and the wherewithal to know right from wrong, up from down and left from right. We have tried to succeed out of our own intellect and schemes and we have failed. We have squandered valuable resources and time attempting this on our own.

We do not always know how you are speaking to us, so keep whispering to us, if that is how you are speaking. Keep shouting at us, if that is how you are speaking. Keep providing significant relationships in our lives, if that is how you are speaking to us. Keep us requiring more of us, if that is how you are speaking to us.

Keep speaking to us until we hear you clearly and do exactly as you command. For you know where we are missing the mark. Our lack of wisdom clogs our understanding and impedes our ability to hear you. May we have ears to hear. May we have the strength to endure and wisdom to keep moving

PERSONAL REFLECTION

How do you define and recognize wisdom? In what areas of your life do you find you need greater wisdom and strength? How will your life differ when you are exercising the wisdom you seek? What are you willing to release so you have the strength you seek?

DAY 2
TRIED ALL I KNOW

My Lord and my God.

Today is a day that I come to you because I understand I have direct access to you. I come to you because I trust that when I come to you that you hear me and you will answer my prayer. Lord, I have tried all I know to try and I do not wish to grow weary of trying something new or different simply because it causes temporary discomfort.

I have relied on the counsel of friends. I have relied on the strength of prayer, and I have relied on the truth that you know me and you want me to experience life abundantly (John 10:10). I have cried all that I can possibly cry and my situation has remained the same. I am frustrated and depression looms. I am frustrated and I am not alone because others are also ready to give up.

I do not have a backup plan. That which I envision in my mind and what I see around me does not always agree. I have loved until it *hurt so good* but I do not feel that

3

same love returning unto me. I have expressed joy so exceedingly that some call me "silly," but joy does not ricochet or boomerang in my direction. I have given up to the point of bankruptcy and my ability to give has outlasted my willingness to give. My wants, hopes, dreams and desires have morphed and evolved beyond my comprehension.

I need you. I need to try something else, something more and something vastly different from the quid-pro-quo approach I mastered. My giving and my getting is not getting it. My spirit is emptying more and more each day. I need you to guide me and to comfort me as I attempt to face the challenge of yet another day. I need you to guide me and confront me as I release more of my ego and embrace more of your way and your character. I need you because I have tried all I know to try.

PERSONAL REFLECTION

What is your definition of love? How have you expressed joy in your life? What is your greatest desire you have for your self right now? What is a hindrance in your life that you can name but will not confront?

DAY 3
DETERMINATION

Give me the determination, the substance, character and passion I need to spend my time wisely and in service to others. Time focused on myself has been well spent and time focused on the needs of others has not risen to the same level of prominence. My calendar does not reflect a needy world. My cupboards do not reflect a world where hunger exists. My phone log does not hint at a world full of lonely and lost souls. Yet, sometimes my heart does.

Having a heart for service that bleeds when others are in pain and a head that aches when thoughts of humans as anything other than beings created in divine and holy images may do the trick. However, there may also be a need for character building, substance and patience. Grant me patience as you help me see others as you would have me see them and enough spiritual awareness to surrender the reservation I have placed on the nearest judgment seat.

While you are at it, help me to see myself in ways that give me permission to envision past my own past, and I can glimpse the good in others as they pass my way. I believe a passion for service will aid me in my quest for spiritual transformation in myself and in the lives of others.

I am willing to let You lead me and guide me in your word. I am willing to let You lead me and guide me in your work. I am willing to let You lead me and guide me in your world. I am willing to let You lead me out of my weakness to a place of determination to serve something more sustainable and meaningful than my own ego. The world is in need of prayer and compassion.

As a matter of confession: I am a part of this world and my attitude and contributions within it are a part of the problem. Yet, with you working in me my heart and life can be transformed by your power and my receptivity to it. I am determined to see that it comes to pass for me.

PERSONAL AFFIRMATION

I can be the change I seek. I will be the better me for the world to see. I shall walk the roads made by people more noble than I. I shall honor the constructs, experiences, and perspectives that cause me to pause. I know I am capable of giving and receiving goodness, kindness and care. I relish in the thought that I have the capacity for goodness flowing throughout my being awaiting kindred and accessible places to connect.

DAY 4
HORIZONS

Lord, help me see and thrive beyond the horizons that others and I have set for my journey. That means I need courage to see beyond the horizon and to accept the variations of reality that exist outside of what I already know or have contrived in my mind.

I want to see more than what I see right now so I know my life matters and what I make of my life matters beyond my existence and inventory. Those whom you have blessed me to know in this life are also of great importance. Their presence teaches me that love and vision require transparency and vulnerability.

As my propensity to reach for higher heights and my desire to strengthen relationships increases, please know I am grateful for how you have held me and shaped me through past experiences. I am grateful for how my experience of your love has shown me how to be more merciful and more gracious with others and with myself.

God, give me eyes to see the bright future you have in store for me and grant me a spirit of optimism when looking ahead.

Help me rise above my own skepticism and cynicism so I might encourage myself and others to look beyond any place and every foe ever known. Find me and banish me from my hiding places.

Help me come out of my shell of self-doubt, my canopy of unforgiveness, my shelter of self-pity, my cave of confusion and my garage of stinking thinking so I can be of great use to you as I look beyond the horizon.

I need to see more goodness in the world and I am willing to be a part of creating and sustaining it for your glory. You can count on me to do my absolute best and not to make excuses for shortcomings and misgiving that shall arise.

Thank you for helping me see that where I am and what I am feeling only amount to experiences along the journey and do not fully define my character or mark my destiny.

PERSONAL REFLECTION

How have you experienced and expressed grace in your life? What are you hiding about yourself that scares you to share it with anyone? Who are you most afraid of losing? What are you most afraid would change if your deepest secrets and desires were ever revealed to a trusted friend?

DAY 5
HOPE FOR HUMANITY

I hope one day, all of humanity, regardless of color, creed, sexual orientation, political persuasion, geographic location, immigrant status or liturgical homeland will be loved, honored and cherished because each one is a reflection and emanation of divinity.

I hope the best of who we are will supersede the worst of what we often see around us. I hope to see people speak up and speak out of their pain without wounding others. I hope all of humanity will live beyond their pain, to forgive themselves, to forgive those who have sinned against them, to no longer be oppressed or to oppress others.

I have hope in humanity that we would all be transformed by the renewing of our minds. I hope we accept that God created each of us and created us in the image that was holy, divine and acceptable, without regard for the labels crafted and placed upon us and do little to tell our stories. I hope all of humanity will release those labels and we refuse to wear them. I hope we will claim our humanity by extending dignity, grace and love to family and foreigners.

I hope that whom God has created us to be as a human family will be made real and manifest in all of our lives through the words we say, through the relationships we build and through the communities we fashion.

May our public voice and our private unctions be consistent, congruent and concise enough to share in a prayer for all of humanity.

PERSONAL AFFIRMATION

All of creation has purpose and that creation includes me. I have purpose. My joy in life is dependent upon how I live out my purpose and fully develop my character.

My character is not a role I play. It is how I show up in the world and has great impact on what I contribute to the whole of creation. I can explore many things in search of my purpose, knowing my character will be shaped by those experiences. I shall not fail in this pursuit as long as I continue moving toward fulfillment.

DAY 6
GENESIS, AGAIN

Lord, hear my prayer, again and again and again.

You know the joy I feel and the pain I have endured. You know the guilt I harbor. You know the tears I have cried. You are the essence of joy I long to know. You know the full desires of my heart. I know you love me unconditionally. That is why I ask you to help me as I begin anew, again.

This is not the first time I have sought a new beginning and it most likely will not be the last time. What I know now is that I must surrender some more of myself for your purposes.

Help me to surrender my will for your will and my plan for your plan. Help me to open my heart to your heart and activate the creativity, spirit of adventure and faith needed to adjust to the necessary changes in my life. I can make it because you are my firm foundation.

I need you to be my unwavering guide, my unbridled strength, my ever-increasing joy, and my enduring peace.

Thank you for loving me and for never, ever giving up on me, even when I have tried to eject and reject you before beginning any change. I may have felt alone as I walked away from you, but you stayed right beside me to assure me you were with me at my first, hundredth, and thousandth step. You are here in this beginning, again.

Thank you for being patient with me. Thank you for bringing me to a point of faith where I know I have to trust you and fully rely on what you must pour into me and purge out of me. This is a new beginning. I have done this before so I know I do not have to fear the unknown. I can begin again.

Thank you in advance for giving life with more than one genesis.

Thank you for forgiving me and for giving me a love exemplified in your willingness to hear my prayer as I begin anew, again.

PERSONAL REFLECTION

Do you really believe God hears your prayers? How do you know you have truly surrendered something to God? In what ways are you certain and willing to admit you are resistant to what God wants for your life?

DAY 7
WEEKLY REFLECTION

On this day it is good to pause and reflect upon all you have prayed and considered the past six days.

This process can be enriched by tracking your thoughts in a journal or with an accountability partner.

If you are journeying with a group, it will be important that one of your ongoing prayers includes something about vulnerability because this process, if taken seriously, will require each participant to be vulnerable about spiritual and personal matters. It will also be important to pray for a suspension of judgment and shame, whether for/about self or others.

One's prayer journey is deep and imperative for a healthy and balanced existence. Any words, gestures, or actions that undermine another or one's own spiritual growth has long-lasting impact and must be avoided and repented at all cost and in every instance.

- A GUIDE FOR PROCESSING DAYS 1 thru 6 -

OPENING PRAYER/MEDITATION

SILENCE *(Listen to your heartbeat for 2 to 3 minutes)*

INDIVIDUAL REFLECTIONS
When times are tough what is your go-to scripture, character, book or text?

If you had to script a title to describe the past seven days, what would it be?

How do you long for the title to change in the next seven days?

GROUP/PARTNER REFLECTIONS
In what ways are you strengthened by praying these prayers alongside others who are willing to be vulnerable about their own needs?

What was one surprising thing that happened to/for you this past week while praying or as a result of your prayers?

What are at least 2 commitments you will make to your group/partner that will support your spiritual growth?

Who is someone with whom you disagree that you will include in your prayers this week?

SILENCE *(Reflect on the commitments you have made.)*

CLOSING RITUAL / PRAYER

DAY 8
MY SOUL

God, I hope you are pursuing me at a much faster pace than the one exhibited in my oft scurry from you.

I pray that you come, and that you find me in all of my places, once more. It is obvious that I do not always take life seriously, especially when I try to hide pieces and parts of my thoughts, words and actions from you. It is as though I am a child again, playing hide-and-go-seek. This time it is not a game but there is counting.

My soul hears you counting the seven days you took to create the world that you use to model how we shall work and take rest. My soul sees the claims in the 66 books of the Bible that you use to teach us. My soul knows of the 40 days Jesus spent in the wilderness that you use to strengthen us. My soul feels the darkness of the three days Jesus spent in the tomb, that you use to raise us up.

My soul hears you counting ever so deliberately, so I can be ready to come out of hiding and stand in plain view of you and your creation, as you created me. My soul desperately needs you to rid me of all that I use to hide myself from you and from the world.

My soul sees you writing something convicting in the dirt in front of my accusers (John 8:1-11). My soul hears you counting my sins no more. My soul hears you counting on me to listen to you, and to learn from you. My soul hears you counting me as one in the number who will proclaim you as my God.

My soul hears you saying, "Ready or not, here am I!"

PERSONAL AFFIRMATION

I may have been afraid to show the world the true me before today and some fear may still exist today. However, I will begin by taking little steps that help me to be more vulnerable and transparent with those closest to me. I accept that all may not be ready for my truth and some may never accept me for who I am. Their words and my thoughts will never change who God created me to be. My words and their thoughts will never change who God created me to be. I can experience freedom and light in this life.

My soul is precious but it is not as delicate as my feelings. My soul is precious and it is more important to my healing than my ego will ever be.

DAY 9
LAST TEAR

Lord, I want to cry my last tear today. I am so sick and so tired of being sick and tired that I do not know what to do.

I just keep crying about how things are in the world. The uncertainty about how things are not in the world keeps me awake some nights and stuck in my thoughts for countless hours.

When I think about the wars and the seemingly senseless killing that takes place around the world to fulfill ill-sought-after power or wealth, I cry.

When I think about the children who spend night after night sleeping on the streets or sleeping in beds where men and women alike take advantage of them because of their vulnerabilities, I cry.

When I see mothers struggling to feed and clothe their children by means that pull her and the children into the gutter of poverty, despair and hopelessness, I cry.

When I see fathers finding more importance in acquiring street credibility than in raising his credit score so he can provide stability for his children, I cry.

When I see young girls fighting to be women and women fighting over a man like young girls, I cry.

I want to cry my last tear today. Can I laugh until I cry instead of laughing to keep from crying? Is that possible?

I believe you know all things. I suppose the problem here is that I will continue to cry until I truly realize that I can do all things through you. You give me strength to be present. You give me strength to be active so I can work for liberation on behalf of the poor, oppressed and neglected.

Lord, I want to cry my last tear today, but knowing what I know, I need the strength that only you can give to allow me to continue this journey…with my tears.

PERSONAL REFLECTION

What reality or calamity in the world breaks your heart? How do you inhale and exhale each day knowing the ills that face this world? With whom can you share this or these realities without fear of retribution or shame?

DAY 10
DISCERNMENT

God, you made me and you know me. You have set my life on a path, and I pray that I remain committed to the way you have established for me.

I appreciate the work you do in my life every single day. I appreciate your nudging in my heart every single day. Although I sometimes doubt whether I am right or wrong, I never doubt your presence and your ability to lead me to the truth or understanding I need to move closer to what you desire.

You know I have difficulty managing my own affairs, so I ask that you grant me the wisdom I need to discern what is my business and what is your business. When I discover it is mine, I pray I will rely on you to get me through it. When I discern that it is yours, I will pray that you will give me patience and grace to let you be God all by yourself.

When I tend others' affairs, I pray that I can be faithful enough to trust you to continue to work in that person's life and situation in the way that you see fit. Also, if unveiling more of your mysterious characteristics limits the ways in which you move me forward, then remain a mystery. What I do know about you works for me and you work on my behalf in spite of my attempts to manage my own affairs. You are always in the midst of my madness, working things out for my good.

So thank you for the work you do on my behalf, openly and in secret. I trust you, God, as you begin to work on me to help me to mind my own business and to stay out of yours.

PERSONAL AFFIRMATION

I am known and I am loved by God.
Neither my antics nor my faults will change who I am
or the love God has for me.
The strength I need shall be provided.
The wisdom I need shall be gained.
The grace I need shall be made available.
The vision I need shall be revealed.
The liberation I need shall be accessible.
The understanding I need shall be unveiled.
The mercy I need has already arrived.

DAY 11

PROTECTION

God, I need you to protect me and to console me as I grieve the beginning of this day. I am saddened by the fact that another day has begun and I feel as though I may not fully comprehend my place in it. I am saddened by the fact that another day has begun and I feel as though I have already failed before I even put my hands, feet, mouth, or words into action. I may be a little anxious.

I need you to protect me and to console me as I grieve the beginning of this day. You have been working on me for a long time. Sometimes I wonder why you spend so much time and expend so much energy to ensure that I have what I need and that I experience life more abundantly.

I had grown accustomed to living life below my means. I had grown accustomed to living my life without sharing the deepest parts of my soul with others. You came along and began a new work in me. You placed me as a priority in creation and now I must place myself as a high agenda item. That is why I grieve.

I grieve because of what is at the heart of my struggle to live this renewed life and to accept this unconditional love you give. I need you to protect me and to console me as I grieve the beginning of this day. I grieve because I know that as you continue to work on me, I will shed more of the old me. Though I understand that more and more of the old me must go each day, I squirrel away parts of the old me. That is also why I grieve.

Under your watchful and protective eye I will no longer spend time alone. I will commune with you through prayer, study and service. I will no longer live life below my means. I will no longer live paycheck to paycheck because the cattle upon a thousand hills belong to you (Psalm 50:10). I will affirm that I am a child of the Most High.

I will trust you to provide my every need. I will no longer seclude myself and my emotions from those closest to me. I will embrace them with my thoughts and shower them with my love. I need you to protect me and to console me as I shed a little more of the old me. Bury the old, inconsistent and inconsiderate me. Make room for the character and presence you need in the world.

PERSONAL REFLECTION

As you consider becoming new and claiming new rhythms for your life, what do you want to hold onto until the very end? Why? What would it cost you to let go of it now?

DAY 12
MORE

The essence of who I am is all wrapped up in who you are and what you desire for my life. Yet, when I look in the mirror I do not see what you see. When I hear my voice I do not hear what you hear. I do not believe there is congruency between what I am doing and what I was created to add to the great tapestry of your creation.

The essence of who I am is so much more than biology but not void of DNA. I am the makings of my parents, extended family, friends, lovers, employee relations and travels around the world. However, I cannot dismiss the scars of past and lost loves, mountains of regret, valleys of despair, missed opportunities and squandered investments no more than I can over-glorify kicked habits, midnight rendezvous, new discoveries or journeys that awed my soul.

I long to be as you would have me be and less of what the world expects. When those around me see me or hear me they do not and cannot do so through your eyes and your ears. They filter through race, ethnicity, economics, politics, psychology, sexuality and what they believe gives them insight into who I am. When you see me you see your image and your likeness. You hear your accent tempered by grace and extended through mercy. You know my shortcomings, my sins, my faults, my flaws, and my scars and you love me more.

The essence of who I am and what I am is all wrapped up in who you are and what you desire for my life. My longing is to be as you would have me be and less of what the world expects. Being less of what I so desperately fight to make real in my life would ease my ability to love what and who you have created.

Help me change my own lens and filters before I hold others to standards I have not yet accepted. Help me forgive myself for the ways in which I have not fashioned my life as you commanded. Help me be more of the me you created me to be.

PERSONAL REFLECTION

After twelve days of thinking about how you view yourself, how different is your view of your current reality? What is the narrative you tell yourself about yourself that you know is not true?

DAY 13
ESSENCE

God, as I pray to you, I need you to help me love you more today. I want to reach out to you. I want and need you to reach up, to reach over, and to reach beyond all the barriers I have set that keep me away from you. Hold me, push me, lift me, and do whatever will allow me to move closer to you.

I have struggled to let go of enough of my pride, and God, I have struggled to let go of enough of my ego, long enough to share this with you. You know all there is to know about me and you promise that you would never leave me, nor forsake me. Even though I have seen you at every turn, heard you call to me before I reached my own dead ends and I have seen and heard you at work in my life, I still try to block myself from you.

It is strangely ironic how desperately I want the blessings, but I find myself sometimes haphazardly avoiding the one who blesses. I want and need to stop doing that. As I think about it, I realize that if the blessings are this good with all of me, and all of my stuff in the way, I can only imagine what it will be when you get me, my barriers, my ego, and all of my stuff out of the way.

So God, I ask you to do what you have to do to get to me. I ask that you do what you have to do to get through to me. I want you to do this for me, so that I can do more for you and for the poor and needy of the world. The essence of who I am is in there and I want that to be what shows up most in my relationships, my conversations, my goals and my achievements.

PERSONAL REFLECTION

How has your love for yourself increased in the past year? Have you ceased self-critique? Can you look in the mirror and offer yourself at least three solid compliments without hesitating? Is what you want others to experience when with you the same as what you say and believe about yourself when you are alone? Or is there a disconnect between what you want others to see and experience and what you say and see in you? What are your three most endearing and enduring attributes?

Dare to write them and share them with one trusted person. Also consider challenging yourself to affirm your most endearing attributes each day.

DAY 14
WEEKLY REFLECTION

On this day it is good to pause and reflect upon all you have prayed and considered the past thirteen days.

This process can be enriched by tracking your thoughts in a journal or with an accountability partner, even if you begin those disciplines today.

If you are journeying with a group, you are aware of the sensitivity and vulnerability required in this process. If taken seriously and as each participant begins to give shape to each prayer, this process will require a suspension of judgment and shame, whether for/about self or others.

One's prayer journey is deep and imperative for a healthy and balanced existence. Any words, gestures, or actions that undermine another or one's own spiritual growth has long-lasting impact and must be avoided and repented upon recognition of such behaviors. This is soul tending that we do for ourselves and for others for the sake of knowing ourselves, each other and our God better each day.

- A GUIDE FOR PROCESSING DAYS 8 thru 13 -

OPENING PRAYER/MEDITATION

SILENCE *(Pay attention to your breath for 3 to 5 minutes)*

INDIVIDUAL REFLECTIONS
What has been your go-to scripture, character, book or text this week?

If you had to paint a picture that told the world the state of your soul, what would be the dominant color? Why?

Is that the color you long for it to be or is there another color you desire to dominate your soul's canvas? Why?

GROUP/PARTNER REFLECTIONS
How are you challenged by praying these prayers with others?

What are at least 2 personal or spiritual discoveries that surprised you this week?

Who is someone you have deemed courageous that you will now offer prayers of gratitude and strength?

What is one thing you are facing that requires prayerful support?

SILENCE *(Reflect on the commitments you have made.)*

CLOSING RITUAL / PRAYER

DAY 15
COURAGE

I am grateful to see another day and to have an opportunity to participate in your creative work in the world. I name my need this day because I do not profess to be cowardice, but I can be complacent and apathetic.

Lord, give me courage to do what you have called me to do and to bring all of my burdens and misgivings to you. Give me courage to hold onto the truths of your word until my change comes. Give me courage to let go of the things that keep me from growing closer to you. Give me courage to stretch my spiritual ear and to open my heart.

I want and need all these things so that I can become better acquainted with you and better acclimated to your voice. I want all these things so I can follow direction that helps me live authentically and courageously at all times.

As I think about your word and I think about how you led Abram to a new and unknown land I realize he had to know your voice and he had to fully trust you (Genesis 12).

I am also reminded of Moses and how he was tending sheep in Midian when you spoke to him out of a burning bush (Exodus 3). You told him who you were. But he had to know something about you in order to accept that it was you. It required courage to trust and to accept your way and your voice, so help me get to that point.

If it is in the whisper, let me hear it. If it is in the wind's crisp breeze, let me feel it. If it is in the falling of sweet morning dew, let me taste it. If it is in the rumblings of the land, let me smell its victory. If it is in the holy scriptures or in the media frenzy of the day, let me see it and know it is from you. I know you can do it and with some courage, so shall I.

PERSONAL AFFIRMATION

I am courageous beyond measure.
My courage is mine for me to use to overcome any fears and all obstacles that appear on my path to wholeness.
I am courageous beyond measure. No one and no thing can limit the courage I have except me and any negativity that I allow to supersede what God has told me about me.
I am courageous and my life will be the manifestation of my courage. Starting now.

DAY 16
TRANSFORM

Great and loving God, help me let go of what I want and begin to praise you and thank you for what you provide, which happens to be exactly what I need.

I know I come to you most often as if I am approaching Santa Claus. I tell you what I want and expect you to deliver it just because it is what I want. I sometimes come to you as if you are a genie. I rub my hands together and expect you to grant my wishes so you can stay in my good graces.

I sometimes come to you as if you are my secretary. I dictate what I want, and you are to figure out how to get it to me by the deadline I set, or by the deadline that is implied in the tone of my voice when I make my request.

I expect you to know my thoughts before I think them. I expect you to know my words before I speak them. I expect you to read my mind. Unfortunately, you do read my mind. Unfortunately, you do hear my words. Unfortunately, you do see everything I do. But fortunately, because of your grace, you also see my heart, and its truest intent.

It is in knowing the intent of my heart, that I know you know that I am capable of being a true and devoted disciple. It is in knowing the intent of my heart, that I know you know that I will get to where you want me to get to. I just need to get out of myself, and get more into you. I struggle with knowing how to stay in this thought once it leaves my mind and my mouth. My consciousness is swarming with my to-do and my should-be lists. Somehow what we agree to in the hallows of these moments do not make the list and when they do they fall prey to the pen that crosses them off for the follies of the day – work, play, advancement, likeability, prestige, power, cynicism, apathy, thoughts of famine and rumors of wars.

Transform me by the renewing of my mind every second of every day so that I stay tuned to the goals of this journey and less enthralled by the wayfarers who mean me no good - even when they are thoughts of my own making.

PERSONAL REFLECTION

Are you currently your best self possible? What are two things you can do to be more authentic and more vulnerable? How will you be held accountable to try?

DAY 17
ISSUES

God, you know my every weakness, and you know how comfortable I am hanging on to what I call my shortcomings, my natural flaws, my serious realities, and casualties of life. You know how hesitant I am to let go and let you take control of every area of my life. I have issues.

What would people think if they knew all there was to know about me? What would people think if they knew I sometimes struggle to do the right thing? What would people think if they knew I sometimes choose to do the wrong thing in advance?

What would people think if they knew that I love you but I sometimes struggle with how you show your love toward me? Would their knowledge of my issues demonstrate that all of us, regardless of our station in life, struggle to find our place and we struggle to let you show your strength through our weaknesses?

Sometimes I do not understand the point of all this. At other times I see exactly what you are trying to move me toward. I am grateful for those times and I am grateful for those glimpses, because they give me the strength I need to do what I need to do for you and in your name. Sometimes my love fails and my excuses do not measure up.

I really want to do better and be better every day. I have made some changes and I see some progress in my life. Thank you!

I ask that you continue to work with me and my issues. Challenge me to trust you, to hear you, and to respond to your call for total surrender. Thank you for calling out to me even when you know I pretend I do not hear you. Thank you for not rejecting me because of my issues. Your love and acceptance is like none other. I love you. Thank you.

PERSONAL AFFIRMATION

I am important and I have grand ideas. There is a vision for my life that I may not fully comprehend, but it is real regardless of my view of current realities. I am important and my life matters to others. I have within me what it takes to be great and make great things happen in my life.

DAY 18
WHOLENESS

You said in your word that when we are sick, that we can "call on the elders and they will anoint us with oil, pray the prayer of faith, and the sick shall recover" (James 5:14-15). Such truth is hard to comprehend when I have family and friends who pray daily for healing and they have waited patiently for a cure.

You said in your word that "by your stripes, we were healed" (Isaiah 53:5). You also said in your word that where "two or three are gathered together in your name, touching and agreeing on one thing, that there you are in their midst" (Matthew 18:20). You said in your word that you would "withhold no good thing from those who walk with integrity" (Psalm 84).

You may have noticed I know your word and I know there are promises of wholeness and healing in your word. The problem is I have figured out how to get the words off the page and into my head, but I have not figured out how to get the words from my head and into action.

I do fine when assuring others of the steps needed for their healing, deliverance, and advancement, but I oftentimes fail at affirming my own faith for a brighter day.

I want to believe that you will heal those who are wounded. I want to believe that you will touch my body, that you will touch my heart, my mind, my soul, and you will take the pain and doubt away. I want to be able to lay my head on the pillow and know you have me in the palm of your hand, and no one and nothing will take me away from you. I need you to give me what I need to let you hold me and to trust that what I perceive as inactivity could be your way of waiting for me to be still and know that you are God (Psalm 46:10). That is what I need.

I pray that what may seem like inactivity is really your way of waiting for me to be still and know that you are God. I pray that what I perceive as inactivity is your way of healing me and making me whole. In the stillness of this moment, speak so that I may know you are God.

PERSONAL REFLECTION

In your experience, is there a difference between healing, wholeness, and a cure? What would be a true indication of your healing or wholeness? Will you accept wholeness without a tangible sign of healing or a cure?

DAY 19
TRUE

Lord, as I come to you I know that often times what I hear in the world contradicts what I know is in your word. I know that in your word I am told to seek after you, like the psalm that said, "As the deer pants for the water, so my soul longs after Thee" (Psalm 42). I also know that Shakespeare wrote, "To thine own self be true." These thoughts are contradictions in my spirit. What am I to do?

I need you to help me to be true to you as I follow your lead. When I slip into thinking that I have it all figured out, quicken me to realize that you have me in the palm of your hand and that is where I shall remain. I want to be true to you so I can be my best self. I want to be true to you so I can be who you want me to be in this world.

I want to be true to you so I can be who you want me to be for this world. I want to be true to you so I can be who you want me to be to this world, in spite of how this world views you or me.

I want to be true to the one who made the heavens and the earth and the one who can count the hairs on my head. I want to be true to the one who loves me with unfailing love and one who gives me life, mercy, and purpose. I want to be true to the one who created me in a divine image and the one who calls me "Beloved." I want to be true to the one who tells me "If I hold my peace, victory shall be mine" and the one who knows I am imperfect and forgives me.

Thank you for the care and compassion I experience in others because I know it comes from you. Thank you for the grace I receive in the midst of my failings and my successes. Your love is amazing in every way. The life you have given me has shaped me and sometimes the world around me and the antics within it cause me pause. However, in my gaze, I am made aware that you are always near the real and truest me there shall ever be.

PERSONAL AFFIRMATION

I am better today than I was yesterday. Tomorrow will bring new opportunities for me to be even better. I can be more authentic and more transparent with others. I can be vulnerable with those who deserve and can honor my vulnerability. I love myself enough to show up in the world and give the world the best of who I am. As I grow I will have more to give and even more room to receive the bountiful blessings coming my way.

DAY 20

FORGIVENESS

As I come to you, I know it is important to forgive those who cause harm. I know I am to forgive those who trespass against me. I know I am not to hold grudges. I know I do not have the capacity to store up all the pain and injustices wrought and rampant in the world. I know I should not hold up the sins of the past, in the face of one who has sought restitution and is attempting to move forward because it holds me back.

David said, in Psalm 51, "...that against you, and you only, have I sinned." I sit here in my sin and realize that I sinned against you and I have also sinned against myself. What am I to do when I am the one who has committed the sin against myself?

What am I to do when I have forgiven others, but still find it impossible to forgive myself? I cannot seem to let myself out of the prison I built of guilt and shame. I know I cannot forget what I did to myself or to others and I may have to live in the shadows of it forever. There may be scars and wreckage that remain long after the offense and restitution, but with your help and acceptance of your grace I can live beyond it and not be consumed by it.

I come to you and ask you, will you do what you have to do to give me the grace needed to forgive myself? Will you do what you have to do to give me the mercy needed to forgive others for sins and acts that question or challenge my humanity and cause me to respond and to live as one with little or no dignity?

As I move into this new way of being and this new way of forgiving myself, please allow me to accept forgiveness, but never to settle for the defeat that comes as I wallow in self-pity - never to settle for the defeat that comes as I wallow in self-loathing and depletion of pride.

Help me say and accept that I am a child of God and I am forgiven - set free to extend grace and mercy to all who yearn for it.

PERSONAL REFLECTION

What is the easiest aspect of forgiving a person who has harmed you? What is the most difficult aspect of extending forgiveness to others? What is the most difficult aspect of withholding forgiveness from yourself? If you are choosing to withhold forgiveness from someone and you are not ready to release them, what is one prayer you can pray for them today?

DAY 21
WEEKLY REFLECTION

On this day it is good to pause and reflect upon all you have prayed and considered the past 20 days. This has been a transformative process.

If you have journeyed on your own, it will be helpful to continue recording your thoughts in your journal and to select a prayer partner with whom you will share some of your future struggles, commitments and learnings.

If you journeyed with a group, it will be important to maintain confidentiality beyond the conclusion of this process. Also include group members and partners in your ongoing prayers. You may consider including petitions about compassion because this process required each participant to be vulnerable about spiritual and personal struggles. It was and shall remain important to pray for a suspension of guilt, judgment and shame, whether for/about self or others.

Any words, gestures, or actions that undermine another or one's own spiritual growth has long-lasting impact and must be avoided and repented at all cost.

- A GUIDE FOR PROCESSING DAYS 15 thru 20 -

OPENING PRAYER/MEDITATION

SILENCE *(Listen to your heartbeat for 4 to 6 minutes)*

INDIVIDUAL REFLECTION
What has been the most enduring self-image this week?

If you had to sing or play a song that told the world the state of your soul, what would be the your song? Why?

Is that the song you long for it to be or is there another song or lyric you desire to dominate your soul's airwaves? Why?

GROUP REFLECTION
What has been most challenging for you praying these prayers with others?

What are at least 2 spiritual disciplines you would like to try this week?

Who is someone you have deemed gracious that you will now offer prayers of thanksgiving and courage?

How will you continue your daily prayer discipline? Who will hold you accountable to continue in prayer each day?

SILENCE *(Reflect on the growth you have experienced.)*

CLOSING RITUAL / PRAYER

Now that you have invested in this 21 day process, you have what you need to craft, create and explore the discipline of prayer on your own. Go pray!

For more information and resources on prayer ministries and leadership empowerment, visit:

2020LeadershipLessons.org

and

CedrickBridgeforth.com

www.ingramcontent.com/pod-product-compliance
Lightning Source LLC
Chambersburg PA
CBHW060622030426
42337CB00018B/3142